Behind the Broken Glass

Kayla Allen

Presentation by *BookLeaf Publishing*

Web: www.bookleafpub.com

E-mail: info@bookleafpub.com

ISBN: 9789358736304

First edition 2023

*To everyone who believed in me and told me
that my poems were good, even when they were
about sitting by my crush on the bus. To
everyone who has loved me through it all.
Lastly, to everyone who hurt me because I took
that pain and made it into something beautiful.*

PREFACE

Some of these poems may be hard to read and
have dark themes.

Untitled

I'm not loneliness but I sleep in her bed
Listen to her voice inside my head
I let her tuck me in at night
When I cry she's by my side

I'm not anger but he lives in my heart
His melody rips my walls apart
He lays dormant while I'm awake
But my sleeping mind he takes

I'm not depression but she's a friend
Coaxing me to the cliff's end
Whispering that no one cares
Stripping me until I'm bare

I'm not anxiety but he's around
Near my heart is where he's found
In my mind he wanders the halls
He hears voices in the walls

I'm not death but she's always nearby
Saying how sweet it is to die
She plays the same song every day
Convincing me I shouldn't stay

I'm not broken but he holds my hand
Pushing me when I try to stand
Some days I don't even try
The hope inside me starts to die

I Could

I could pass by the eyes of millions
And still remain unseen
I could own a dress in every color
And still they wouldn't see

I could be the kindest person
And still not have a single friend
I could save the lives of billions
And still be lonely in the end

I could sing the greatest love song
And still not say a single word
I could paint the greatest pictures
And still be a cage bound bird

I could show the world my broken heart
And still they'd insist it was beating
I could hand everyone a band aid
And still they wouldn't stop the bleeding

Ghost of You

Some nights the ghost of you visits me
Kissing my lips as I sleep
Somehow I can't seem to say goodbye
To the secrets I promised I'd keep

Some nights I'm desperate to call you
To hear your voice in real time
Somehow I know it'll do me no good
You've already left me behind

Some nights the ghost of you haunts me
And I ask it how you've been
Somehow I know it'll tell me lies
Yet I miss you all over again

Some nights I wish I could call you
And ask if you still love me
Somehow I know that the answer is no
But my delusion is so lovely

The nights when the ghost of you haunts me
I can never turn it away
I let it climb into my bed
And pretend that you had stayed

Meadow

Take me to a meadow
Speak softly and sweetly
Tell me how you love me
How it changed your heart to meet me

Take me to a meadow
Open up your chest
Let the secrets tumble out
Lean on me and rest

Take me to a meadow
Hold me oh so near
Let the wind's quiet chorus
Tell us what we need to hear

Take me to a meadow
Let me wipe your tears away
Tell me all your secrets
I promise that I'll stay

Soundtrack

If my life had a soundtrack it would be
The sound silence makes as you fall asleep
The sound of a flower petal hitting the floor
The gentle click of a closing door

If my life had a soundtrack it would be
The sound of kisses trailing me
The sound of clothing being ruffled
The sound of whimpers that are muffled

If my life had a soundtrack it would be
The stillness of a library
The careful flipping of a page
The whispers of people of every age

If my life had a soundtrack it would be
The sound of music blaring loudly
The thud of drums that matches my heartbeat
The guitar chords that ring inside me

If my life had a soundtrack it would be
The sound of feeling lonely
The stillness of the dark that lies ahead
The sound your heart makes when it's dead

If my life had a soundtrack it would be
A symphony of agony
Before suddenly the music swells
And ends with the sound of funeral bells

Beauty

I have seen beauty in many ways
I see it each and every day
In the glow of my friends' smile
In the river that stretches for miles
In the puff of smoke from a cigarette
That dances toward heaven in a pirouette
In the laughter of the ones I love
In the puffy clouds that float above
In the darkness of the world at night
Where the moon is the only source of light
In the bustle of the city
Whose evening lights are oh so pretty
In the deer that graze along the road
In the croaking of a giant toad
In the caress of someone I hold dear
In a picture of someone who isn't here
In the tears that flow when things are bad
In the comfort given when I am sad
In the music I play in my car
Where I sing loudly and drive so far
In the middle of my darkest day
When someone stops and asks if I'm okay
In the shower burning hot
In the flowers growing in a pot
In the mountains of Yosemite

In the roaring of the sea
In the strangers that I see
Chatting with their families
In the uniqueness of those I love
In the things you're ashamed of
In the way you snort when you laugh hard
In a hamburger perfectly charred
In the conversations I overhear
When they don't realize I am here
In the eyes of everyone I've met
Where so many untold stories rest
In the games that children play
In the pain that doesn't go away
In the silence people leave behind
In the darkest corners of my mind
In the swaying of the trees
In a refreshing summer breeze
There's so much beauty I can see
I can finally see it when I look at me

Untitled

I wake up alone
Startled by the chill in the dawn air
My hand absentmindedly reaches
To the pillow where your head used to lay
If I make it to a thousand years
May I never love again

I wake up alone
Cuddling my phone again
Reading the messages we sent before
Picturing you typing them and laughing
The distance between us is a thousand miles
May I never love again

I wake up alone
Every night for a thousand nights
And it'll be a thousand more
While you wake up next to her and kiss
I've been up for hours craving your touch
May I never love again

I wake up alone
Remembering the promises that we made
In the stillness of the night
Laughing at our inside jokes
I haven't laughed for months it seems
May I never love again

Lighthouse

I'm a lighthouse by the sea
A lonely woman lives in me
All night long she paces the floor
Waiting for love to knock on the door

The rainy weather brings her cheer
For in the rain you can't see her tears
She drinks cocoa by the fire
Companionship is her desire

She's a lighthouse keeper by the sea
Questioning her sanity
As the days turn into years
She comes face to face with her fear

Inside a lighthouse by the sea
Music plays so softly
The woman dances all alone
Humming in a pleasant tone

As day slips into night she creeps
To her bed to get some sleep
After tossing and turning all night like the tide
Her feelings bubble over inside

In a lighthouse by the sea
The woman, shaking violently,
Follows the stairs up to the peak
With teary eyes she makes the leap

I'm a lighthouse by the sea
With a for sale sign outside of me
For my owner washed up on the shore
She isn't lonely anymore

My Mind

In the darkness of my mind I hide
Praying no one looks inside
For if they love me they'll get hurt
Casualties when my universe bursts
Wounded by stars falling out of my sky
Remnants of wishes I've made that have died
Blinded by supernovas exploding
Earthquakes in sync with my heart rate slowing
Bringing tall buildings to their knees
Hurricanes raging in my seas
Volcanoes erupting like blood from my wounds
Bystanders crushed by my fragmenting moons
Tornadoes ripping homes from the ground
My soul screams - an earth shattering sound
Temples and pyramids crash to the earth
Fire leaps out from the hearth
Lightning strikes down from above
All because I fell in love
So in the darkness I continue to hide
Praying no one looks inside
I stare out over raging seas
And dream of the day I'm finally free

Show Me

Show me again where the brokenness lives
So that I might find a home
Show me where the door opens with a creak
So I can be alone
Show me where the darkness hides
So I might get some sleep
Show me where temptation whispers
Truths that cut so deep
Show me where anxiety plays
On a playground with broken swings
Show me where depression nestles
A baby bird under a mother's wing
Show me where the tears fill oceans
So I can finally drown
Show me where the blades are sharpened
So I can stop letting people down
Show me where the breeze is icy
A sharp slap in the face
Show me where the lilies bloom
So I can see my resting place
Show me again where the brokenness lives
So I can hug an old friend
Show me a life without me in it
So I can welcome the end

Touch Me

Touch me
Not on my skin
Not on the delicate curve of my spine
Touch me deeper
Touch the part of me that's quiet
Like a snowy December night
The part that's untouched
Hiding and afraid in the dark
Touch the part of me that's broken
A glass vase shattered on the floor
The part that has been hurt before
And has kissed death on the lips
Touch me
Not on my skin
Not on the memorial of past abuse
Not on the bruises that only I can see
Long since healed but still aching
Touch the part of me that needs it
That shrinks away and cowers
Touch that part that is afraid to be loved
Afraid to make itself known
Touch the part of me that silently begs
The part that reaches out gingerly
The part that's just waiting for you to
Touch me

Watermelon Kisses

Watermelon kisses under a summer sky
I barely notice time ticking by
Lazily lounging in the backyard
In a haze of brown eyes and blue skies

Sweet sunset kisses on the lids of your eyes
A gentle hand resting on your thighs
Another hand on the back of your neck
My heart is beating out of my chest

Flaming hot kisses when the sun goes down
Against the wall barely making a sound
Hands roaming and finding, teasing and
touching
Unable to control the searing blaze

Sensual kisses together in the dark
One hand on your face, one hand on your heart
The world stops spinning, it's just you and me
Under the stars and blankets cuddling

Goodbye kisses, sad and sweet
You hold me close before I leave
I turn to go, you pull me back
For two more watermelon kisses

What I Want

You didn't ask me what I wanted
So I'm telling you instead
I want to be the one you can't forget
I want to be stuck inside your head

I want to burn you to the ground
Have you roasting in desire
I want you tied up to my bed
While we die inside the fire

I want to drown you in remorse
Regretting that you didn't kiss me
I want to hold you underwater
Until you admit you miss me

I want to play on the radio
Until my voice is all you hear
I want to sing a siren's lullaby
And not stop until you're near

But out of all the things I want
There's one thing that stands above
It's to be by your side for always
And to be the one you love

Untitled

I'm sorry for the compliments I never gave
I'm sorry for the people I couldn't save
I'm sorry for the words I never said
I'm sorry that my heart is dead
I'm sorry I wasn't a better child
I'm sorry I let my heart run wild
I'm sorry that I got bad grades
I'm sorry that I misbehaved
I'm sorry I couldn't give enough
I'm sorry I couldn't accept your love
I'm sorry I played my music too loud
I'm sorry for leaving without a sound
I'm sorry for the pain I caused
I'm sorry for the love I lost
I'm sorry I wasn't a better mom
I'm sorry I couldn't recite the Psalms
I'm sorry for when I was the bad guy
I'm sorry for when I made you cry
I'm sorry for the demons in my head
I'm sorry that part of me wants me dead

It's not about the compliments you pay
It's not about the lives you save
It's not about the words you say
It's not about your heart's decay

It's not about your inner child
It's not about you running wild
It's not about your average grades
It's not about when you misbehaved
It's not about how much you give
It's not about rejecting my gift
It's not about how your music sounds
It's not about when you stopped coming around
It's not about the pain you caused
It's not about the love you lost
It's not about your parenting style
It's not about the Holy Bible
It's not about when you were wrong
It's not about crying all night long
It's not about the demons in your head
I'm just happy you're not dead

Kiss Me

Kiss me
Need me desperately
Like I'm oxygen
Hold me until you're shaking
Breathe life into my aching soul
Push me against the wall
Paralyze me wordlessly
Whisper that you want me
Flush against my skin
Murmur into my neck
Dig your fingers into my hips
Show me
Wrap your hand around my throat
Tell me what you want
Fill my ears with your sounds
Brand my skin with your teeth
Biting until the skin turns purple
Then kiss me again
Drown me in adoration
Show me that you own me
Take me
Throw away fragility
Love me like the world will end
If we don't fill our needs
Grab my hair and pull

Remind me why I'm yours
Watch as my body falls apart
And then comes back together
Let me make your world shatter
I'll worship at your altar
On my knees in prayer
I want to hear you reach the pinnacle
To feel you cross the line
After all is said and done
Don't forget to kiss me

Depression

Creeping up to me in the night
You catch me unaware
Silently you slit my throat
With no one around to care.
You're there in the darkness
Lurking all around
Cutting the happiness from me
Without uttering a sound.
You make me hide from my loved ones
And cry all night long
I hide inside my home alone
With you tagging along.
You nag at me at work all day
Saying I'm a burden
To shut my mouth and not feel a thing
And that will stop the hurting.
I have no friends because of you
I always leave them wanting
Loneliness, my oldest friend,
You're always here and haunting.
You kill me in the stillness
Slowly pushing me around
Turning happiness to sadness
Holding me under until I drown.
The sun sets in the sky again

Time for you to come and play
To have your fun and leave me broken
With nothing left to say

Hush

Hush little baby, don't utter a word
Your cries will always go unheard
Your mommy won't sing you a lullaby
and daddy's not here to kiss you goodnight.

Hush little baby, please don't cry
Don't let them know you want to die
They'll take you away again
To padded cells and imaginary friends.

Hush little baby, close your eyes
If you just fall asleep it'll be alright
Then pain will cease, you'll have friends again
But your fragile life will have to end.

Hush little baby, don't make a sound
There's darkness lurking all around
Give in to its tempting caress
Leave this life and start the next.

Hush little baby, it's time to be still
Grab the bottle and drink your fill
Go to the roof and try to fly
While singing this beautiful lullaby.

Falling

Falling for you would be easy
Like breathing in that refreshing gulp of oxygen
after being underwater
Like watching the wind kiss the grass
Like touching something smooth after rubbing
sandpaper

Falling for you is like waking up
Or sliding into a bubble bath
Warm and inviting, comfortable and calm
A pink and orange sunrise peeking over the
horizon
The face of the sun lighting me up from the
inside out

Falling for you is dangerous
Like taming a lion and swimming with sharks
Like a taser aimed straight at my chest
An unseen branch underfoot when hiking along
a cliff
An exchange of power from me to you
With one kiss you could hurt me

Falling for you is like starting a book

Unsure of the ending, enchanted by the
beginning
Devouring the pages unable to look away
Just one more chapter, one more piece of the
puzzle
Slowly getting invested in your life, pictures
flickering through my mind

Falling for you would be so easy if I let myself
If you let me, I would let go
Fall off the ledge and pull you in
But for now I'm on the sidelines
Waiting for permission to release my grip
To fall into you the way I fall asleep
Slow and then all at once
Steady and sure, like breathing

Untitled

If I had water
Just a little
I'd hold myself under
Until the bubbles stopped coming
Just to dull the pain

If I had fire
Just a little
I'd hold it against my skin
Until it stopped hurting
Just to dull the pain

If I had water
I'd swim so deep
I'd look up at the glimmering surface
Relax my arms and legs
And I'd finally dull the pain

If I had fire
I'd walk right in
I'd let the flames kiss my skin
I'd finally let out all my screams
And I'd finally dull the pain

Outside

I'm on the outside
Looking in the window praying for a glimpse
Of the inside
Where they've got smiles on their lips
I'm an outcast
Begging to be let in
To the circle
Just let me come inside
I'm a figment
Of the imaginations of my friends
I'm a ghost town
It's like I don't even exist

Round and round it goes
I want in and then I don't
Round and round I go
I have friends and then they go

I'm on the inside
Seeing you out there wanting in here
But I can't help you
You see rules are rules
And you're an outcast
Not welcome in here
You're a figment

Of my active imagination
You're not like us
You're a burden
I don't want to open the door
You'll stay on the outside

Round and round I go
I want to help and then I don't
Round and round it goes
You need saving and I won't

Phantom

In the stillness of the night
A phantom holds me oh so tight
His kiss a whisper on my lips
His fingers rest upon my hips

Once the sun has gone to bed
My phantom comes with eyes of red
He won't love me in the light
He only shows up late at night

He waits until I'm fast asleep
Then into my bed he creeps
He whispers that I am his dream
He tells me that he'll make me scream

If I ask to see him in the day
He will surely run away
My phantom only wants to play
He won't respond to what I say

He sleeps beside me every night
But always leaves at morning light
I should tell him to stay away
I'll tell him another day